A MEMOIR

MÉSHELLE FAE

A MEMOIR

Life in Poetry

The Writers' Block, LLC

Copyright © 2020 by MéShelle Fae

All rights reserved. No part of this book may be reproduced in any manner whatsoever without written permission except in the case of brief quotations embodied in critical articles and reviews.

First Printing, 2020

To: Mom & Dad & Teddy

CONTENTS

Dedication
v
Preface
xi

I

Space

Am I Woman?
2

Black Like Me
5

Daughter Of Prometheus
10

I Belong To America
12

Mermaid Tails: A Pantoum
15

Black Love
16

Chicken Little
20

CONTENTS

II

Family

Momma's Pride
24

Daddy's Girl
27

Documentary Of Divorce
29

Sonnet 1: Sisterhood
31

III

Love

When We Make It
34

Beauty And The Beast
36

Worthless
38

IV

Life & Death

I Have No Fear Of The One Called Death
42

The Graveyard Is My Favorite Place
44

Freedom
45

Southern Fried Haiku
48

CONTENTS

My Disney Manifesto
50

The Elegy I Should Have Written
52

V

Legacy

Letter From The Bridge Builder
56

On Owning A Business
58

I Also Dream A World: A Response To Langston Hughes
59

A Teacher's Heart
61

A Letter To My Stars
64

Acknowledgements
67
About The Poet
71

PREFACE

Writing this poetry collection was hard.

A memoir is best defined as a collection of memories (or the retelling of an event) that has enough bearing on someone's life that they felt the need and desire to tell other people. Memoirs oftentimes have more impact than autobiographies because of their brevity and poignancy. They have a focus. They offer some kind of clarity. Each story, or *moment*, is carefully chosen to deliver an audience one message, much like each finger is carefully curled to deliver one punch. I believe that I succeeded in delivering that punch. Sometimes, it was an unwanted jab straight to my gut. At other times, it was a mighty blow to the heaviest burdens I was still choosing to carry around.

I've been blessed with a life well-lived. I am not so young and arrogant to believe that there aren't more lessons to learn. Indeed, looking at my life at almost thirty, I am more excited about what I see before me than I have ever been.

PREFACE

However, that does not mean I can dismiss or forget the hills I have climbed and oceans I have crossed to arrive where I am today. I put together this collection because there are others asking the same questions and experiencing the same hurts that I did. Writing my memoir and expressing my past and present through a series of poems required a lot of mental walking. I had to walk back into the past, into those memories that have been pleasant as well as those that I preferred to forget. All of those experiences created this book. So, I am grateful to the Lord for this opportunity to share this small piece of me in the hopes that it will offer comfort or joy when someone else needs it most.

Furthermore, I chose poetry because I have always been a poet first. I love poetry in all her ways. I highly value and respect the art form as well as feel indebted to every poet I've ever read or heard. It was through poetry that I first learned how to be true to myself. For as long as I can remember, poetry and oral traditions have most often been the more natural (true) form of self-expression for *me*. So, it was an easy decision, or rather compulsion, to present these *moments* via poetry.

Therefore, I chose diverse forms of poetry for this book. From free-verse and persona poems to pantoums and sonnets, I have explored all of my ideas through many of my favorite forms of poetry. I created five 'frames' through which I viewed my experiences and organized the poems

PREFACE

that came out of that introspection: space, family, love, life & death, and legacy. Fair warning: this book, like much of my life, reads like a wild experiment.

So, thank you for taking part in my story - *in these moments* - with me. I hope the lessons I've learned (and my earnestness to give them to the world) touch you, enlighten you, and revitalize you.

Gratefully,

MéShelle

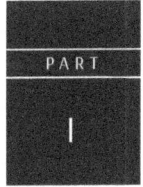

PART

I

SPACE

Space explores the challenges of literally 'taking up space' in today's society. These pieces are about what it has meant for me to be a person who exists with a voice, goals, and a body in a world that often attempts to deny my right to any or all three. As a woman (especially one often viewed as overweight) and as a black person (specifically a black woman), I know what it is like to be made to feel as though my existence is immaterial, a hindrance, or a threat.

AM I WOMAN?

I was born with hips
wide enough to span oceans,
breasts the size of the moon,
a belly shaped like a mountain
and a fertile valley below.

So, they say I'm a woman.

I was born with hatred for
skirts and dresses
nail polish on my fingers
makeup on my face
and being told what to do.

So, was I still a woman?

I grew up with
a need for books and thoughts,
a fascination with sex,
faith in a forgiving God
and a love for pet rocks.

So, was I becoming a woman?

I grew up on
playing video games alone,
wrestling and fishing with daddy;
beating the neighbor boys at football,
and getting dirty with strays.

So, did I act like a woman?

I grew up
being told I was a girl
looking like a girl
feeling like a girl,
and didn't know what girls
were, looked, or felt like.

So, what was a woman?

I became
someone's play toy.
someone's afterthought.
someone's girlfriend.
someone's wife.

Now, am I a woman?

I began to love
"throw-on" dresses
books about magic

books about sex
going to church
the color of nail polish
farting in public places
sitting with my legs open
sex in public places
tigers, cats, dogs, and snakes
friendships with other women
stories about faith
debates about sex
discussions about race
and arguments about womanhood

Now, who is a woman?

I am.
I am the leader of the pack.
I am the best choice.
I am a bad decision.
I am brown sugar and honey.
I am the dirty fighter.
I am the beast, not the beauty.
I am the burp when you're full.
I am a Slytherin and a Hufflepuff.
I am selfishness and cruelty.
I am sacrifice and giving.
I am an adventure.
I am the journey.

I told you I'm a woman.

BLACK LIKE ME

how would I feel?
how should it be?
if my daughter is born
Black Like Me.

what would the world
think of she
this daughter of mine?
Black Like Me.

if her father be black
or if her father be white
or someone they tell me
just ain't quite right

would my daughter be theirs?
or would the world only see
my little girl as being
Black Like Me.

Black like the roots
of the tum tum tree
where Jabberwocky trails lead
to cinnamon trees, oak fields, and
bronze wheat grass.

Black like the past
Black like the atlantic ocean
where Black bodies
formed the sediments
on their way to form the settlements
of their future and our present
self-celibacy

will my daughter be
Black Like Me
and have no love for
the person in the mirror
because mommy said
don't talk to strangers.
that's the danger
when my daughter is
Black Like Me
not white like them
and not dark like her
and not light like him.

already marginalized
living outside the majority
then she'll be separate and unequal

within her own minority.

mommy is my black black?
or is my black brown?
is it new york or southern?
from up or downtown?

is my black african, caribbean, latina?
is my black indian, native?
is my black european?

how should I feel?
how should it be?
asks my daughter
Black Like Me.

what does the world
think of me?
asks that daughter of mine
Black Like Me.

is my black black enough?
for me to get by
mommy you didn't cover this
in your poems and your lullabies!

i don't know who i am
who i was
who i should be

so what does it mean to be
Black Like Me?
my history is stolen
my now is subverted
mommy my
post-racial society
lives on the wrong side of the tracks.
and i'm told who i am
is how i should act.

so who am i?

baby girl I don't know it all
but I know what I believe
and I believe your Black is
as Black as you want it to be.

the world will define
your identity as they see
so don't ask them
tell them
who you choose to be.

and if you still don't know
then please watch and follow me
because i'll show you how
to be
my queen
Black Like Me.

[This version was adapted from its original slam poem style. Slam poetry refers to poems written specifically for oral performance (usually without props, costumes, or music) at artist events, open mics, or competitions known as poetry slams. It was awarded 2nd place at a poetry slam the year it was written.]

DAUGHTER OF PROMETHEUS

That's our light they stole...

Run like fire
Daughter of Prometheus
Don' let Zeus
an them boys
catch you here.
Hair a-curlin'
Like great balls of fiyah!
Bring that torch on here!

Run like fire
Daughter of Prometheus
Don' let Hera
an them gurls
catch you here.
Curvy hips and curvy thighs
Not near they husbands!
Not this time!

Run like fire
Daughter of Prometheus
Don' let Hades
an them boys
catch you here.
Bad as baby brotha
White sheets over they eyes!
We need yo' light my dear!

Run like fire
Daughter of Prometheus
Do yo' po' daddy
an them
proud.
Skin bronzed
It's been a hard day's journey,
Run on home now!

Run like fire
Daughter of Prometheus
Let yo little light shine
on us all!
Don' let the eagle catch you a' day
Don' let 'em have they way.

That's our light they stole…

I BELONG TO AMERICA

America is my mother.

So excited to start this new family.
Before postpartum depression set in.

Now all we can share
are broken promises - homemade,
like slices of apple pie
baked under fifty stars.

America is my father.

Determined to be better
then his daddy,
but sadly comes up short.
So suddenly,
"You ain't none of mine."

I'm not yours!
I was born to you, America!

I didn't choose!

I look like your child:

Red undertones in my skin
from Georgia clay
where blistered Cherokee feet
marched in tears
carrying history on their shoulders.

White palms and nails
from the original immigrants
looking for fountains
and stealing youth
under Florida palm trees.

Brown skin and lips
from southern belles
who *cruised* on slave ships
so the birth of a nation
could drip from their sweat.

I don't need the paternity test.

Illegal and illegitimate are not the same.
I have your broken DNA.
So why?
Why don't you want me?

You hide me from the mothers and fathers
of your favorite children.

You send them sweet gifts on Christmas,
and celebrate them on birthdays.

Do I look like your mistakes?
Do *they* look like your achievements?
Because we're all broken inside
from being inside of you, America!

Why? Why? Why?
Why do you give me kicks for kisses,
and punches for hugs.

I have changed the world
to please you.
I have damaged the world
for your attention.

I have changed myself
to please you.
I have damaged myself
for your attention.

And *still*, you deny me.

Well, one day I won't need your love.
One day, I won't ask for your permission.
One day, I will take my inheritance, America.

And you'll belong to me.

MERMAID TAILS: A PANTOUM

Mermaids are NOT what you call beautiful.
Spare me the stories, the legends, the hype.
No need for choruses or refrains; our souls are musical.
Far too big to be true to size.

Spare me the stories, the legends, the hype.
Our bodies have no gaps or lean places.
Far too big to be true to size.
We reflect the Divine's many faces.

Our bodies have no gaps or lean places.
This is more than your artists can render,
We reflect the Divine's many faces.
I want you to always remember:

This is more than your artists can render,
No need for choruses or refrains; our souls are musical.
I want you to always remember:
Mermaids are not what YOU call beautiful.

BLACK LOVE

I want to save Black Love.

She's on the endangered species list:

Destruction of territory
where gentrification
'white' washes old neighborhoods
and family plots.

Climate change
where single-parent households
teenage births and
high school dropout rates became normal.

Increased poaching
as private prisons
and street corner graves
thin the population.

Over-exploitation
on reality TV shows
as housewives and preachers

create the illusion of "real."

Invasive species
in movies, magazines, and YouTube ads
as black beauty is portrayed as
rough, scandalous, enslaved.

This loss of biodiversity
has cut off most
opportunity for
repopulation and growth.

All efforts towards conservation
have met reservations
budget cuts
and a lack of public interest.

Black Love isn't cute
and cuddly. It
won't play fetch. It doesn't
do well in cages.

And there's nothing wrong with
White love
Chicano love
Asian love
Indigenous love
or Mixed love.

Those populations are my Least Concern.

They are public - like a Frog.
And I don't disavow their Love.

But
Black Love is my favorite.
I celebrate Black Love.

Growing up uninformed:
I watched the powers of this world
set traps for Black Love
then hide their hands.

For the sin of our skin
we were forced to ask forgiveness
from the world.
But we only needed it
from ourselves.

So, I forgive you, Auntie
when you said,
"She's gonna marry
a white boy."
Who hurt you Auntie?
Was it Black Love?

Black Love
Self Love
is a form of healing
and resistance.

So, I seek contributions
to create awareness
and build an environment
where Black Love
can thrive.

CHICKEN LITTLE

I wish I'd known I was a chicken.
I might have acted responsibly
if only someone had told me.

Chickens are good.
People like them.
Breasts, thighs, and legs are
Popular.

Chickens lay dead eggs
without any need for consent.
Chickens make baby chickens
without being told.
Such convenient pets?

Little wings can only
carry chickens over fences.
But not to freedom.
Delicious aren't they?

I wish I'd known I was
Supposed to be a chicken.

I wish I'd known that was
Their purpose for me.

But I once saw an eagle fly

I always knew
I can fly too.

So I would jump
and fall;
I would jump again
and fall.

Chickens can jump rather high.
So my thighs get better with each jump
And my breasts get larger with each breath
And my legs get stronger with each fall
And my wings get wider with each try

At sunrise, I was a chicken.
Thank God I didn't know it.
At sunset, look to the west,
and watch me...soar.

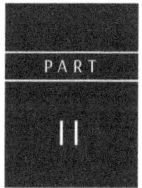

PART

II

FAMILY

Family has always been more than a word to me. It's a lifestyle and a choice. Family manifested in my life in the form of a double-edged sword, contributing to both my greatest victories and deepest wounds. Still, I wouldn't be here without them. The greatest lesson I can pass along, however, regarding family is this: Not all blood is family, and not all family is blood.

MOMMA'S PRIDE

momma is a proud woman
standing tall at five foot five
nothing and a half
with a momma bear sounding
boisterous laugh.
she's a novel, unwritten
she's cheesecake, unfinished
she's truths yet spoken
she's a cross worn, but not broken

momma is a proud woman
 her Bible is her shield
her tongue, a sword
she is a dahomey warrior
amazonian queen of old
and da homies knew not to mess with her
so they did what they were told.

momma is a proud woman
unafraid of her blackness
unafraid of her womanhood
proud of her femininity

in an age rampant with white male dominance
and toxic masculinity
momma's pride is a symbol
of all of our dignity.

momma is a proud woman
before she was his bride
that other one's bride
someone's sister
that one's lover
momma was still a woman
even after she became a mother.

and through rain or shine
whether sick or well
through downs and ups
when it felt like heaven or hell
momma is a proud woman

and i'm proud too
to be raised by a by a legend
as proud and beautiful as you.
before i had pride of my own
i had yours
it was big enough
to open all my heart's doors

when she said,
"that's momma's pride
reading that book

for the first time.
walking on that stage.
gliding down that aisle.
smiling at the sun.
laying on my breast.
that's momma's pride
pushing me to be my best."

"that's momma's pride,"
she'd tell me with a kiss.
"that's momma's pride.
look at her.
there she is."

[Mother's Day 2018. Adapted from original oral style.]

DADDY'S GIRL

My Daddy makes things

like dad jokes
friends wherever he goes
and salmon patties for breakfast.

My Daddy transforms things

like car engines
the old shed in his backyard
and a lullaby version of "Rapper's Delight."

My Daddy builds things

like his own hype
his own business
and his relationships with his daughters.

My Daddy treasures things

like his favorite cigars
that new motorcycle smell

and finding the perfect fishing spot.

My Daddy sees things

like what a person needs
how hard someone works
and straight through the bullshit.

My Daddy owns things

like his pride
most of his mistakes
and the right to be who he is.

DOCUMENTARY OF DIVORCE

lights. camera. action.

flashback
8yr old girl laughing
a *meet cute* with Mickey at Disney
parents biding their time
before the truth comes out

in medias res
8yr old girl crying
a mother's breast is soaked
a father stands silent
a warm room gone cold

red herring
16yr old girl ranting
on the inside
why should she be angry? they ask
no vows were broken to her, they say

foreshadow
23yr old student dating

like she's on defense
carrying her past around
like foul play

anticlimax
28yr old woman writing
a passive-aggressive poem
just to say
the shit still hurts

SONNET 1: SISTERHOOD

My sisters taught me a song about us.
The chorus matches pace with my heartbeats.
Rhythmic flow like blood pushing gentleness.
Our memories are notes on music sheets.

The sound of laughter pours from each refrain.
This song crescendos with each passing year.
Lyrics spill tales of our secrets and pain.
The deepest smiles have harmonized with tears.

Our song can rock and roll with broken strings.
It spits bars--drops beats in feminine tones.
It 'Lady Sings the Blues' like the Queen.
Its soulful timbres resonate in my bones.

I wish to teach the world our melody.
Only no one hears it but them and me.

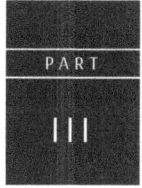

LOVE

Love needs no introduction...

...but it's always nice to start a new chapter.

WHEN WE MAKE IT

I won't just look for
vacations on days
that end in "y."

I won't just look for
3.2 children, 2 dogs,
and a savannah cat.

I won't just look for
rolling hills, a lake,
some trees and a stable.

I won't just look for
2 guesthouses and a west wing
for 3 sets of parents and grandparents.

I won't just look for
jam sessions on
starry nights with
overstamped passports.

I won't just look for
what you promised me.

I'll look for your hand in mine.
And smile for you.

BEAUTY AND THE BEAST

He is the beauty:
calm, cool, collected.
He sees the mysteries of the world
and answers them in kind.

I am the beast:
wild, passionate, unabashed.
I see the truth of the world
and rebel against its inequities.

He is Persephone:
sacred, willing, yet pulled.
He chooses my darkness with
every chew of the pomegranate seed.

I am Pluto:
raw, powerful, still alone.
I envelop my love in the richness
of my bounty and need for his touch.

I have become a cannibal
for my love,
consuming my own depravity
for my love,
until all that remains is a cavity
for my love.

I. have. almost. confused.

emptiness --
for light.

WORTHLESS

Worthless can be quantified.

It's the age
I first called myself fat

It's the price
of innocence
after my first porn at 8

It's the amount
of tears
after their divorce

It's how many times
he looked at me
in total disgust

It's the number
of nights I cried quietly
to escape mom's worry

It's the tally

of men I needed
to call me beautiful

It's the sum
of people I allowed
to tell me who I am

It's the word count
of lies I could stomach
in one day

It's the percentage
of myself
I could admit to liking

It's the fraction
of me
left after a breakup

It's the cost
of a scholarship
I lost twice

It's the calculation
of debts
on my credit report

It's the total
of my fingers-
too few to count my failures

It's the product
of a life
brimming with bad decisions

It's the chances
of me being convinced
that I'm anything but perfect.

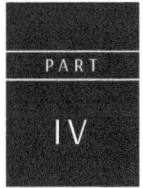

PART IV

LIFE & DEATH

Life and Death are the great equalizers in that they are the common denominators shared by all humanity. They are also intricately connected. One gives presence to the other, just as light is needed to cast a shadow. At some point, one's body is alive, and, at another point, it is not. The pieces in this section explore the feelings, thoughts, emotions, and conclusions I've drawn from my experiences with and contemplations on the two.

I HAVE NO FEAR OF THE ONE CALLED DEATH

I have no fear of the one called Death
He holds no mystery.
For He and I are a mated pair;
We share long history.

He has always loved me
since before my birth,
and for my presence he has longed.

In truth-

the desire for His touch
has my body e're only known.

But Death, my Love estranged
must take others to His bed,
Lest Patience be His undermining,
instead enduring friend.
For I have a lover all my own
who guards me jealousy.

And Life has fickle young affections;
his caresses, light and carefree.

I know our summer's eve

burns bright

burns fast
the wind upon the sea;
But at dawn's light my lover
surely shall abandon me.
And my true Love,
shall take my hand
as we always planned to meet -
my Guide to the Son
to my eternity.

THE GRAVEYARD IS MY FAVORITE PLACE

the graveyard is my favorite place.
the finish line, the end of the race.
it holds no lies, no deceit.
it's where we all must one day meet.

only here will enemies find their peace together.
only here will men lie in equal weight and measure.
only here will differences not cause strife.
here is where most men will celebrate their life.

the graveyard is my favorite place.
though it knows no language, it speaks of grace.

FREEDOM

You were there
in the soft white light of
summertimes gone by
on snowy Panhandle beaches

There
on weekday afternoons
PS1s - blowing
on Nintendo cartridges

There
in my first Harry Potter book
magic wand
and a knack for trouble

There
in mama's arms
daddy's laugh
grandma's cookin'
auntie's eyes

You weren't there

in college
the first job
the last job
my first time

You weren't there
when he sat beside me
at the restaurant -
so he wouldn't
have to look at my face

You weren't there
when she told me
"they set you up."

You weren't there
when I was locked away
the girl in the mirror
said, "Throw away the key,"

but I couldn't.

Because you came back
I left him
I found her
her new voice

When you came back
I wrote another poem
and it told the truth

When you came back
I met my husband
I loved my husband
he loved me

Do you remember?
Nina said
what you meant
to her:
"No fear."

SOUTHERN FRIED HAIKU

Sweet Potato Pie

'erb, root, sum 'nilla
ma'dea secret respees
good kich'en magic

Yad Chik'N/Yard Chicken

cluk'a cluk'a cluck
carolina summer nights
lovin' cock in da mo'ning

Sunday Mo'Ning Dancin'

right foot. left foot. clap.
chests just a'bouncin' up down.
(soles) is bein saved.

Black Woman Problems

chirren's an men folks
meetins wit da womans board
dem hours well spent

Sistah Connection

strangers lined in rows
sundresses on layaway
where'd you buy dem shoes?

["Sistah Connection" was a featured piece in the South 85 Journal Spring/Summer 2018 issue. It was published online on June 15, 2018.]

MY DISNEY MANIFESTO

Every girl is a princess, and a princess can choose to be president. My mistakes don't define me; my responses do. **Be nice to everyone, including your toys.** Whether it's at first sight or after many encounters, love is scary, confusing, and wonderful...all at the same time. **Hakuna Matata is more than a motto.** All I need is a little faith, trust, and pixie dust. **Sometimes, I'm the villain of my own story.** I can write my own destiny. **I can change my family's story.** Not all nightmares are bad. **Let go of any person or place that makes me feel less than magical.** My conscience will always be my guide. **Have some imagination.** Take all offers for magic carpet rides. **Earth is my Treasure Planet.** There's nothing wrong with wishing on stars, but I've got to back it up with some hard work of my own. **This girl's greatest weapon is her dream...and a frying pan.** Let it go. **Being a hero isn't about what I do on the outside; it's about who I am on the inside.** The first lesson: find balance. **Family comes in all sizes, shapes, colors, and species.** At some point, we've all felt like a fish out of water. **Don't be afraid to go into the Unknown.**

There's still a little magic left in the world and in all of us.
There's always the chance for a remake.

THE ELEGY I SHOULD HAVE WRITTEN

(Rest in Paradise Aunt Shelia)

She lives over there, deep in the wood.
Those are *her* purple orchids you know.
That bark you hear comes from the trees
where ancient waters flow.

The river's edge laps soft and still,
its heart a rush of waves.
Lavender lotus blossoms rest on lily pads
as perfumed floating graves.

She gave the ferryman two pence
for safe travel past her dreams;
Her smile he carried across waves of mauve
in his boat and coat of aubergine.

There is no pain, deep in the wood.
There is no slow decay.
Seraphims climb milky skies,
on sextet wings of violet shades.

Clouds of periwinkle in the morn,
diamond stars at night,
white and lavender ribbons adorned,
when she took her ferry ride.

It was with consequence she left
to go where we could not abide.
Despite her own heart's desire,
the wood has no room for those outside.

These bowed, unbroken souls she left
still speak fruits of love on her name.
Her scent, much like sweet amaranth,
still lingers throughout our days.

The wavy vines and curly limbs,
she once wove with violaceous hands?
Have they been tended with such loving care,
since she met her ferryman?

The laughter she suckled at her side,
has it e'er been heard again?
Or did it follow her, deep in those lilac woods
to linger with its true friend?

Pray tell, where is she now deep in the wood?
That her loved ones may yet find
a pomegranate seed to chew
and not be left behind.

They reach the outer bank at last.
She finds the carafe of mulberry wine.
She waits for us beyond the wood
atop a bed of thyme.

[Honorable Mention - 2018 Baltimore Science Fiction Society Annual Balticon Poetry Contest. It was published on page 62 of the 2018 Balticon 52 Convention Booklet.]

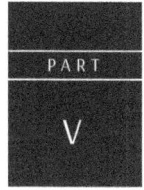

PART

V

LEGACY

Legacy is the greatest gift we can leave in this world, both for others as well as for ourselves. The legacy we leave as individuals and also as a generation is so important. The richest place in the world is the graveyard, where dreams, visions, innovations, and life-altering ideas have gone to die with people we should have known existed, but do not. My goal is that, at the end of my life, if I have a tombstone, it reads: "Used up." When the Lord calls me home, I pray that I've left every gift, talent, ability, and opportunity He gave me here on this plane for someone else to benefit. That way...my heart stays here after I'm gone.

LETTER FROM THE BRIDGE BUILDER

You will not forget me when I'm gone.
For what I've built today,
will live long past our settled dust,
to guide you on your way.

For what I've built today,
you may forget my name and face.
To guide you on your way,
follow where my hands and feet were placed.

You may forget my name and face,
but you'll never know how treacherous was the tide.
Follow where my hands and feet were placed.
You'll know the marks I've left you as your guide.

But you'll never know how treacherous was the tide.
You won't stumble in the path that swallowed greater men than I.
You'll know the marks I've left you as your guide,
as you cross safely to the other side.

You won't stumble in the path that swallowed greater men than I.
It will live long past our settled dust.
As you cross safely to the other side,
you will not forget me when I'm gone.

[A pantoum-styled, persona poem inspired by the renowned piece "The Bridge Builder" by Will Allen Dromgoole, a fellow Southern Belle poet.]

ON OWNING A BUSINESS

Must be quite the vice?
I've now done it thrice!

I ALSO DREAM A WORLD: A RESPONSE TO LANGSTON HUGHES

I dream a world of children
No children are left behind

Where bookbags and backpacks
Are booked for soccer practice
Packed with love

There is a person called home
A place called, "Mine"
And love says, "You're *enough*"

I dream a world of children
And no reduced lunch line

Mommies and Daddies make bread
Bring home the turkey bacon
And there are little pigs in blankets

Happiness is gluten-free
Laughter is organic
Family time isn't microwaved

I dream a world of children
The guns are only Nerf

Just sticks and stones break bones
Words are the only WMDs
Hands go up for high-fives

Girls are strong and weak
Boys have laughter and tears
And it's ok to tell the difference

If only the world could see
What I see in the world I dream

A TEACHER'S HEART

I tell my students
it's good to see them

but I mean it.

It's so good to see
boys in school
not being dragged in cuffs
from Starbucks

It's so good to see
girls in school
not escaping in the night
from slavery

It's so good to see
boys in school
not firing a gun
at innocent people

It's so good to see
girls in school

not under the hand of a friend
whispering #MeToo

It's so good to see
boys in school
not stolen from parents
at the border

It's so good to see
girls in school
not denied their dignity
for wearing Boricua shirts

It's so good to see
children in school
not suffering violence
from their masters - I mean- caretakers

It's so good to see
children in school
not hungry at home where
cupboards lay bare of hope and food

It's so good to see
children in school
not in sick beds and hospitals
praying for one more day

It's so good to see
my children in school

where I can keep
them safe-

even if it's only until 2:30

So, I tell my students
it's good to see you

and I mean it.

A LETTER TO MY STARS

i have journeyed;
through the calmest night of my life
in a place of serenity
crowded by patience and virtue
darkness cut by the light of the moon
night songs played by cicadas
fresh air chilling the heat on my skin

i have known
peace
acceptance
joy
love
and have named them after you

for you are stars to me
guiding lights above
that remind me of where home is

for you have been a resting place
a solace from the seas
a place of learning and laughter

before the map read
before the course plotted
before the sails unfurled
before the anchor raised

i will laugh and learn with you
now

the moon rests
the Son appears
the light shines
but behind the clouds
my stars twinkle on

ACKNOWLEDGEMENTS

Thank you, Jesus! Thank you so much! We finally made it!

Woot! 30 poems for 30 years (counting the back cover!)

This book ultimately became a catalog of the journey I took to find myself. It is also the physical manifestation of the journey to find my voice as a poet. I remember, with painful clarity, the many days filled with doubt about myself and my work. There were moments when I was not sure I would finish. But faith has seen me through. I am so happy...with the finished product...with the pride of finishing something I started (at last!)...and most of all...with myself. However, I could not have gotten here alone. If you are not listed here, please, as we say in the South, "charge it to my head and not my heart."

Thank you Anna Marie Rhodes for hours of countless editing and never blessing me out when I would call last minute because you "have to help me read over just three

ACKNOWLEDGEMENTS

more poems!" Without you, I would not have confronted half of the demons I needed to slay to achieve this book.

Thank you Dr. Corel Lenhardt for the encouragement and accountability, whether it was a call, a text, an email, or an impromptu trip to Atlanta. It all proved valuable for us both in the end! Also, thank you for allowing me to be unapologetically black, woman, all-natural, and educated in your presence.

Thank you Robert Ligon for loving me through this process. Your silent touch and whispered encouragement went a long way towards helping me see this through to completion. I love you, Teddy Bear!

Thank you Mama for all those years of journals and notebooks as gifts. You knew what was happening, even when I thought that you were just being excessive.

Thank you Daddy for being such a great cheerleader and checking on your baby girl. I am always encouraged when you ask me, "What's the dill pickle? Is everything kosher!" You're great.

Thank you CLC for telling me I could do this ten years ago and badgering me until I did.

Thank you Ms. Fredrica Terry (Mama Dukes) for telling me

to finish ONE THING. That was the greatest request I think anyone has ever made of me.

Thank you Grandma Linda Faye and Aunt Tonya Michelle for your names. A name is a powerful tool and an impactful declaration. It speaks to who you are. I appreciate the loan.

Thank you Ms. Kenya Greggs, Ms. Cece Jordan, and Dr. Patrice Williams Shuford. Good teachers are actually not hard to find. However, great role models and influencers in AND OUT of the classroom are another matter. Ms. Greggs, I was in the 3rd grade when you taught me the immense importance of being true to myself and my ideals. Thank you so much. Ms. Jordan, you made me write my first poem in 5th grade at 10 years old, and winning that county-wide contest gave me an 20-year confidence boost. Thanks! Dr. Williams Shuford, you were the first English teacher to make me read beyond the words and redefine the power and impact of writing. You also redefined for me the power and impact of appreciating life. You once casually told me about life, "I like it here." At that moment, I had such a visceral reaction because I realized for the first time how much I like it here too. Thank you.

Thank you to my Orlando Poetry community. Love you guys so much for the wisdom and memes you freely offer. I am so appreciative of how many amazing poets I witnessed during my college years. If it weren't for how self-conscious

ACKNOWLEDGEMENTS

you made me with your 'realness' and greatness, I doubt I would have worked so hard to get better!

And most of all, thank you to you. Yes, you! You gave my book a chance to live beyond my hands. Without you picking up this little book, these words would be lost. I owe you a debt of gratitude, and I am taking the time to express it now. Thank you. Thank you. Thank you. You did not have to buy it, pick it up on the street, steal it from someone's purse, or lose a dare. But you did! So I am thankful for the opportunity to share my story with you, however that opportunity came. I hope this encourages you to tell the world your story as well. We need it.

Gratefully Again,

MéShelle Fae (www.meshellewrites.com)

MéShelle is an overindulged millennial born in Atlanta, GA. She's a daughter of the American South and currently lives in Charleston, SC with her husband and an overactive imagination. MéShelle is a Baltimore Science Fiction Society's 2018 Balticon Poetry Contest Honorable Mention. She is also the author of the forthcoming *Goddess Quartet* New Adult, dark fantasy series. Her work has been published in "Fiction Southeast" and the "South 85 Journal." She loves Disney, comic-book films, and anime. MéShelle has a passion for teaching, mentorship, and community activism.

As a YA to Adult speculative fiction writer and a poet, MéShelle writes for the nerds, has-beens, geeks, almost were's, weirdos, and defects. She writes to tell our stories and deliver our truth... *with a magical touch.*

A Memoir: Life in Poetry is her first poetry collection.

www.ingramcontent.com/pod-product-compliance
Lightning Source LLC
Chambersburg PA
CBHW070303010526
44108CB00039B/1793